Surviving

Surviving

How we loved through pancreatic cancer

K. Blake Cash

authorHOUSE®

AuthorHouse™
1663 Liberty Drive
Bloomington, IN 47403
www.authorhouse.com
Phone: 1-800-839-8640

First published by AuthorHouse   08/04/2011

ISBN: 978-1-4634-3889-0 (sc)
ISBN: 978-1-4634-3888-3 (ebk)

Library of Congress Control Number: 2011912811

Printed in the United States of America

Front cover: Our wedding rings © 2011 K. Blake Cash
Back cover upper: Blake and Emma © 2002 Willis Cash
Back cover lower: Blake's last look at 10th and Wolf © 2011 Godelieve Monnens-Cash

This book is printed on acid-free paper.

In loving

memory of

Amelia Mary "Emma" Aquilino-May-Armstrong-Cash

Dedicated to

Godelieve Monnens-Cash

The women who taught me more about loving

than I could have ever imagined existed

Prologue

I think about beginnings. Some are clear, finite, moments I'm certain of; others are hazy, sometimes indecipherable. The universe began with light, whether you believe God said, "let there be light" or you believe that a vacuum fluctuation allowed the existence of a single photon. But what was before that? With no energy, no mass, there could be no time. What was here before? It simply doesn't matter.

I met Emma in person on a certain date. I spoke to her on the phone before that, and responded to her personal ad even before that. But in some ways, I had always known her. It simply didn't matter what was before, and when she left, it took some effort to realize that my universe would continue without her.

The origin of her ending is just as difficult to pinpoint. I can identify the end of the beginning of the ending relatively easily, but the beginning of the ending could in many ways be said to have been the beginning of all time, the twisted path determined by the orbit of the first electron. Other thoughts imply responsibility, and I cannot blame anyone or anything for life, nor how the experience unfolds.

It is only natural that this beginning is hazy.

Emma and I had both been in long relationships before we married, but neither of us had ever been married to one partner for ten years.

Our tenth anniversary was a goal she looked forward to with more anticipation than her fiftieth birthday. She thought about it for almost the entire preceding year.

We were living in South Philadelphia, a few blocks from where she had spent her early years, where much of her family still lives. It was a comfortable existence, she found work in the numerous local restaurants, and most recently she was the chef at a café two blocks away. We took public transportation everywhere. She had never driven a car, and I had stopped driving a few years before we moved to Philadelphia. We were friends with many of the local shopkeepers; it was in many ways an old world experience.

About this time (I prefer to remember it as being after the actual anniversary), she began to complain of discomfort in her kidneys. Emma never visited the doctor. She had watched her mother die, and like many people, associated medicine with death. Even though I have no faith in medicine, and had given up entirely on treatment of my own Multiple Sclerosis, I still found myself being the one to suggest she see the doctor. I tried to convince her that problems were easier to fix if they were small; waiting could allow irreversible damage. I was aware that even though we were only just past fifty, we could no longer think we were invulnerable. Emma was stubborn and could never admit weakness, which is what she thought illness was. So we waited. She complained of the growing pain, but sought no treatment.

The jaundice I finally noticed in her eyes was something she could see, something she could not deny. We made an appointment to see our doctor. He initially thought she had contracted hepatitis; the doctor had an experience with the local grocery store's prepared foods and thought that was the source. Emma was furious. Her mind often went in impossible directions, she thought I had somehow brought hepatitis home and given it to her. We spent the nights before her appointment without intimacy, as she went from blaming me to trying to protect me from infection.

The doctor did some blood work, and prescribed an ultrasound to look for any blockages in her liver. We were only four blocks from a hospital so I suggested we get the test done on the way home. In the twisted path of life, this may have been the most important casual decision we made about her treatment. When we arrived at the hospital, they told us we would have to wait three weeks before she could have the ultrasound. I wasn't crazy about this particular hospital anyway, and Emma had always preferred Jefferson hospital, where she had fertility surgery when she was younger. I had taken the day off from work, so we decided to catch the bus and go to Jefferson, which was only half an hour away.

While they did the ultrasound, I waited in the anteroom. Emma always claimed to be psychic; I do know that she was very perceptive. She picked up something from the radiologist; somehow she knew something wasn't normal. She asked to see the doctor who interpreted the findings by herself. She loved drama.

Emma had an exceptionally strong will coupled with a forceful personality. She smoked, and as public opinion became increasingly anti-smoking, she smoked more. Her mother, whom she idolized, died of lung cancer. Her mother still smoked even after having a lung removed, while in the hospital receiving oxygen. When restaurants started prohibiting smoking, we would just stop going to those restaurants. When the law made all smoking in public places illegal, we stopped going out to eat. Emma always said her food was better than what we found dining out, which was true. When we had visitors who didn't smoke, the normally overly hospitable Emma would make it a point to smoke in our small apartment.

Emma came out of the consult looking exceptionally serious. She was scared, but could never admit it. She told me we'd talk outside, that **I** would need a cigarette. The only other thing she would say is "It's bad". She said that several times. We got outside, and lit cigarettes. "It's cancer, I have pancreatic cancer", she said. She looked at her cigarette and said, "I guess this is my last one of these" as she tossed it to the ground. That's when I knew that she was truly scared.

I knew there was no way she could have received such a diagnosis in the few minutes she had been with the doctor. "What exactly did he say?" I asked. "There's a mass in my pancreas," she said. "So he didn't say it was cancerous, it could be anything" I said. "It's cancer, I know it." And that was all there was to it, she knew, there was no arguing.

The mass was blocking a duct from her liver to her pancreas, so she was scheduled for a stent to be placed in the duct via a procedure called an ERCP (Endoscopic Retrograde Cholangiopancreatography, we quickly started talking in acronyms) in which a tube is inserted orally to reach the liver. I didn't know such a path existed. This was our introduction to being patients in the hospital.

We were admitted through the ER, there were more images to be taken so she was NPO (non per os, Latin for "nothing by mouth", in practice, no food). The admissions process took us into the late night, and the images were not taken until around noon the next day. While the doctors scheduled the stent placement, she remained NPO. By the time I arrived from work they still hadn't decided if the procedure would be done that evening, and she was STARVING. The blood work had shown blood sugar problems. One nurse in particular couldn't get it through her head that Emma was not complaining because she was a diabetic with no impulse control, she was diabetic because her pancreas wasn't working properly due to the mass. She needed food because she had been NPO for over 24 hours.

Following the procedures the variety of specialists increased, the level of communication did not. We heard about diabetes, but no commitments on whether or not she actually had diabetes, and from the point of view that she could control it with diet. When the word "cancer" came up we got our introduction to "Shoe inspections", which is how we referred to the way the doctors would stare at their shoes instead of the patient.

When we got home we spoke to our primary physician, he sent a prescription for insulin to the pharmacy. Emma's second husband had diabetes, so she was familiar with testing blood sugar levels and injecting insulin. We had a few problems in the beginning since stress is also an issue in blood sugar control. It was over a month before we could see an endocrinologist.

We saw the surgical oncologist the next week. In the interim she had more CT scans. She really hated CT scans; that is, she hated the contrast fluid that she often refused to drink. She spent most of the week telling me how she would not take chemotherapy because she couldn't stand to be sick; how she wouldn't take radiation because she couldn't stand to lose her hair; how there was no way she would undergo surgery because that would only spread he cancer. We didn't sleep much, she was troubled and tossing through the nights, I was troubled and worrying through the nights.

The surgeon told us that from the level of cancer markers (CA-19-9), and the appearance of the mass (they still weren't calling it a tumor), it appeared to be cancer. We were given a treatment plan: chemotherapy, radiation, surgery, and more chemotherapy, over the period of about a year. We were told that we were "lucky", we were in the small group (four percent) of patients who were even eligible for surgery. The possibility of survival was present.

It took us some time to define "survival", to learn to decipher "doctor talk". Our first task was to decide if we would pursue any treatment at all. Emma's attitude towards doctors went into hyperdrive. She often said she wouldn't accept any treatment if she ever had cancer, so now that she did have cancer she wasn't going to back down.

That was the end of the beginning. Two months had passed since our tenth anniversary. That's how this story begins.

June 2009

Emma always kept me on my toes, from our first meeting right through today, which is almost a year after her passing. It took quite some time to find her changes+ comforting, knowing that her uniqueness was what I loved. When we were facing a terminal diagnosis and she couldn't decide whether or not to receive treatment I found it maddening. Something told me she would follow through, she investigated a number of treatment centers, spoke with survivors (the fact that we found just two in the entire country seemed to bother only **me**), and went to appointments for imaging and consultations. I knew her, she needed to be in control, and being told what to do was not within her definition of being in control. She had stated since I first met her that she would never undergo cancer treatment. She had a fascination with death, and yet she was also full of life. Emma loved the experiences of the moment, and the expectations of the future. **More**. She always wanted more. Right now she was in pain, and more life meant more pain. I understood her dilemma.

When we entered the doctor's office I had no idea what her decision about treatment might be. She was cranky about having to fill out the paperwork (this would continue, a year later "cranky" was far too polite a term). Then God gave us a gift. Dr. Yeo, the lead surgeon in the group, a world famous pancreatic cancer surgeon, guided us to the examination room. This moment, his demonstration of humility, is what I believe cleared Emma's mind. She saw him as a person and not a

7

figure in an ivory tower. When our surgeon Dr. Lavu spoke to us Emma was involved, not just listening. She then said the words that are most precious in my memory. She said "I want to live".

The appointment with the chemotherapy oncologist, Dr. Avadhani, was two days later. More paperwork (anyone facing prolonged medical treatment should ask for a photocopy of the paperwork they fill out on an office visit, and just hand that in each time). It's the same form, but no two doctors share files, very shortly it becomes annoying to answer the same questions over and over. Dr. Avadhani was young, female, and had a positive attitude. Emma's chemotherapy would be in two phases before the surgery. First, Gemzar once a week for a few months, then Fluorouracil (aptly called 5fu) by pump, 24/7 for five weeks. Dr. Avadhani was able to prescribe medication for Emma's nausea and pain. Emma told her that if she didn't start chemotherapy right away she'd back out. I knew Emma was brave, but I had rarely seen her so in touch with her feelings, acknowledging her own fears and weaknesses. Later in the day I discovered just how fragile she was.

It was clear to Dr. Avadhani that Emma was scared, and she recommended that Emma see a counselor. Dr. Lavu had done the same, as had I. Emma thought only crazy people see a psychologist, and she wasn't going to accept that she needed this kind of help.

I took Emma home and went to work. Later in the day the chemotherapy department called to verify her appointment to begin treatment the next week. Emma called me in a panic, now it was real. It was as if she had just received the diagnosis, she was horrified. By the time I came home with the prescriptions, she had moved on to anger, trying to find someone to blame for this. I was an easy target, so I let her vent her frustration on me. I was able to get her to take a Dilaudid and an anti nausea pill. With her pain went her anger and she fell asleep rather quickly. I went online, and started searching for support groups not only for patients, but for care givers. I also started a website to document the experience. At the time, I was thinking about how we could look back on this together after it was all over. It seems natural that I was optimistic then. In hindsight I can tell you that I remained optimistic; obviously less about long term goals, but I never gave up. Not even in her final hour.

She slept well, with vivid dreams no doubt brought on by the medication. She woke up hungry, something new, but angry again. While I was in the shower she went for a walk, a habit she had began a few weeks earlier in an attempt to control her blood sugar. I began to worry a few hours later when she hadn't returned, and started calling around. After four hours I called the police, they arrived just as she did. I had been worried she might have decided to end her life, she had spoken about it as an alternative to the indignities of chemotherapy and radiation. Of course she blew it off to the cops, saying she had been at church, but I did get across to her that I cared and that I was watching.

Monday morning we had another CT scan. Dr. Avadhani had ordered this one before chemotherapy could start on Wednesday. I mentioned earlier how much fun Emma was when it came to CT scans and contrast fluids. Tuesday we got a call saying that the chemotherapy had been postponed. There were nodules found in her lungs. **Now wait just a minute,** if the nodules are cancerous, they would be treated with the same chemicals as the pancreatic cancer. If having cancer someplace else

K. Blake Cash

was a problem why wasn't a scan including her lungs done earlier? I'm the level headed one here and now I'm starting to get pissed off, this is a setback she was not prepared for. Emma now had a reason to refuse chemotherapy again, she said that if there was cancer in her lungs then it was a sign from her mother. I am crushed by a feeling of hopelessness, "No hay remedio". The only way to be certain about the nodules would be by needle biopsy. We watched the video of the procedure together and I had to agree with her, even I wouldn't go through that.

After a miserable week, we received Dr. Avadhani's opinion of the CT scan. She had gone over it with several radiologists. There was a seventy five to eighty five percent chance that they were just cysts or scar tissue related to Emma's smoking, and not cancerous. The truly good news was that Emma could see this as good news, she was developing a sense of perspective. She was once again looking forward to beginning chemotherapy, now scheduled for the following Wednesday.

Now a brief word about the price and payment of healthcare in the United States. We received a phone call from the hospital's billing department asking us to sign up for welfare. I have rarely been so insulted. It seems that they didn't think our insurance would cover all their grossly inflated charges, and wanted to recover all they could. They even had hospital employees who would facilitate our signing up for welfare, and gave us a sales pitch on all the benefits. Our first stay at the hospital, when the stent was placed, was $30,000 for just the hospital room for two nights, not including all the peripheral services like the ERCP to place the stent, or the images, or the consultations. Insurance paid $10,000 under their agreement with the hospital. Had we been on welfare the hospital would have collected a higher percentage. In the first year of treatment our gross medical bills totaled nearly one million dollars. I understand why the hospital would have liked to collect more than a third, but I found this move to be despicable. A few phone calls and sharp words were enough to get the billing department to leave us alone. In fact I never heard from them again outside of their billing statements.

With the scheduling of chemotherapy, the nodules in her lungs declared safe by Dr. Avadhani, Emma's mood improved. The night before her appointment she was feeling good enough to cook, which for Emma was always a production. As much as it brought her joy, it also took a lot of energy. She made rollatini, and I was able to enjoy a bottle of Chianti I had purchased thinking I would need to calm myself the night before her first chemotherapy. I did not need to calm myself, Emma was in an accepting mood. She knew she might not be well enough to cook and was joking about how I should pay attention because she would expect the same quality dishes from me. She made love with me that evening, something that had been missing from our lives. Though now I can see that she may have just been resigned to her fate, at the time I read it as being positive and excited about moving forward.

She insisted on going to the infusion center on her own, and agreed that I should meet her there after her treatment and bring her home. It is these memories that tear me apart as much as her weakness did later. She was always strong. Despite her fear she soldiered on, making conversation with other patients, even making new friends. Emma felt best when she could share her strength with others, she was outwardly healthier than the other chemotherapy patients.

She was exhausted, but had a good appetite by dinner and went for a walk with me afterward. She slept fairly well, even though we had an appointment for the next morning with the radiation oncologist and she hated having more than one hospital trip a week. She was up in the night to be sick only once, we had expected much worse.

The next day we met the radiation oncologist, and once again filled out the entry paperwork. Neither of us liked the people in radiation. It's funny how certain departments have distinct personality traits shared by everyone who works there. I've noticed a similar trait in office buildings. Sometimes everyone uses the revolving doors while in other buildings everyone avoids them. The doctors in radiation oncology were distant. The more of them we met the more they reinforced the impression, I never bothered to remember any of their names. Emma would receive radiation therapy five days a week once the second chemotherapy drug began. At least radiation was impersonal enough that she wouldn't mind being there every day; that is to say she didn't mind enough to complain about it. She would need yet another CT scan to mark the points for radiation, so that gave her something to complain about. She was in a good enough mood to joke with other people on the bus home.

We had both heard the horror stories about chemotherapy and radiation. Emma was a beautiful, youthful woman, who at 52 could pass for under 40. She was proud of the care she had taken of herself and did not want to lose her hair or have her skin wrinkle. Nausea seemed unavoidable though. We had a prescription for Marinol, a marijuana derivative that allegedly worked wonders through chemotherapy, but when I brought the prescription to the pharmacy it might as well have been on fire. The pharmacist backed away and said "We don't carry that, you'll have to go somewhere else" without touching the piece of paper. The conventional anti nausea drugs that she took caused constipation, as did Dilauded, so we put aside the anti nausea drugs because the dosage of Dilauded was being increased. Not enough to make her hazy, she wanted to feel some pain to remind her she was still here, but 4mg was a higher dosage than the first pharmacy I visited had in stock. None the less she weathered the first week much better than we had expected. She was starting to feel warm, partially because it was summer in Philadelphia, and since she thought she might lose her hair anyway she had me cut it for her, very short, the day before her second infusion.

Emma did so well the first week she wanted to do the second week's visit by herself. She took the bus in and back home alone. Having a couple of people compliment her hair helped her mood, and she had dinner waiting when I got home. We took our walk together, and she only took half a Dilauded before collapsing for the night. She was pushing herself as hard as she could, and the smile on her sleeping face was reassuring to me.

The next step would be on Friday. We would meet Dr. Berger, who would install a "port". A port is positioned just under the skin, and connects via a catheter to the vena cava, so that each chemotherapy treatment doesn't require a fresh puncture and veins don't collapse. Sounds great doesn't it? In theory it's elegant, in practice it depends on humans. The first step, having it installed, depended on a man with the bedside manner of a hyena. Well, I haven't met any actual hyenas, so I hate to insult them.

Having met approximately a dozen doctors in the last few months, we were certain that Jefferson hospital knew enough to put the nice ones in the window. The radiation oncologist was just distracted, uninterested in her patient. Dr. Berger was arrogant. He needed to be respected (cleaning the spaghetti sauce from his white coat might have helped). He began with interns conducting the interview, then came in and asked the same questions in front of them so he could point out what they had missed. Then he needed to explain the procedure to a patient (Emma, who was already annoyed) in a fashion designed to further insult and instill fear (he was probably reaching for awe). I would have preferred another surgeon, Emma would have preferred to not have a port at all. We scheduled the surgery for the next Wednesday and ended the month on a down note.

We had several friends whose kindness touched us throughout our ordeal. Joey had a way of showing up when things were low and cheering us up. We owed Joey some money. When I called him to ask him to stop by and pick it up, he told me to keep it and take Emma out for dinner. Joey had a number of medical issues in his life, and had learned when it was time to step back and relax. Emma trusted him enough to take his advice, so we went to dinner at Marra's, a local Italian restaurant (okay, that was redundant, almost every local restaurant was Italian). We had antipasto, calamari, and gnocchi. Emma even compensated with extra insulin so she could have dessert. We had a nice walk home, it was a cool evening, and she slept well, talking in her sleep about tartufo. The next day was another dose of Gemzar, and the port was scheduled for the day after (she still hadn't committed to going through with it), but for the moment she was at peace.

The port installation avoided being a complete disaster only by resulting in a functioning port at the end of the procedure. Emma would not commit to going through with the procedure until the morning, although it was clear from her preparations that she was going to have the procedure. She was just resisting. Her nerves had sent her blood sugar through the roof. She had been told not to take insulin before the procedure, so when we showed up her blood glucose was 200 (it should have been closer to 100, mine runs near 70). There was a pre-surgery bathing kit that Dr. Berger's office had failed to inform us about, so the staff was frustrated with us. Then they had trouble starting the IV, it took four attempts total by two nurses. After the third try I had to step in and say that if the fourth try failed I was ready to scrub the operation. Emma was starting to crumble, all her anger and fear turning into defeat. After she was taken to pre-op I settled in the waiting room. A nurse came for me, my heart dropped. She was okay, they hadn't realized that she had body jewelry (both nipples and clitoral hood) that needed to be removed. Give me a break, there was no need to remove these rings. I went back to pre-op and removed them for her. She had refused to allow a nurse to take them out. She was beaten, she looked at me so sadly, and in the weak voice she had left said "I've been stripped of everything". I didn't cry in front of her.

I asked if I could wait in recovery, I wanted to be there when she woke up. That, of course, was against procedure. I hope it was the same nurse who denied my request who had to deal with her when she regained consciousness. Emma's greatest pride was her beauty, one big reason for resisting the port was that she didn't want to have "tubes sticking out of me". She had stopped screaming by the time I was brought to recovery, but she was seething in anger. "I look like Frankenstein!" she said, "I'm going to kill myself!". There were no tubes sticking out, but the swelling around the port made it stand out, making a bump about two inches in diameter and at least an inch tall. There was an incision above the port and one on her neck where the catheter that connected to the jugular had been inserted. I wasn't certain, but Emma was a proud and determined woman, so I made the tough choice and embarrassed her even more. I told the nurse Emma was suicidal. I knew Emma well enough to know that she would never admit to threatening to tear out the port or commit suicide. She calmed down, her new mission was to prove me wrong. At this moment she hated me. I had talked her into this disfiguring surgery and embarrassed her by publicizing her pain. Her immediate reward would be in proving me wrong and not hurting herself, **MY** immediate reward would be her proving me wrong and not hurting herself. It took about three hours for her to realize that. By evening we were holding each other, eating Chinese food and back in love, both of us glad that there was nothing else scheduled for two weeks. We spent a quiet holiday weekend. Emma didn't care for fireworks as they were yet another reminder of her first husband, their anniversary was July 4th.

There's a saying a friend used to describe police work when I worked for a department in Delaware County. "Days of boredom punctuated by moments filled with adrenaline". The next two weeks went gently, our days of boredom. We were on a break from the Gemzar, and the appointment with the Endocrinologist was finally happening just after chemotherapy resumed. I was able to focus on work and we fell into a schedule, a routine. Emma, despite the pain that was only obvious by her consumption of Dilaudid, was walking the neighborhood, proud of how healthy she appeared.

One rainy Sunday she couldn't take estimating her dietary intake any longer, and insisted that I go out and buy a scale. I took the bus up to the Reading Terminal Market where there was a kitchen supply shop open. Emma was coming to grips with her dietary restrictions. Her anal retentive side had her weighing everything she ate, measuring the time of her meals with a precision not applied to train schedules, and walking three times a day. Something was working, her blood glucose was amazingly stable. I think a lot of it had to do with the reduced stress. "Reduced" is a relative term.

When she started chemotherapy again, they used her port. We were warned it might still be painful. Dr. Avadhani had given us a prescription for Lidocaine, but hadn't been clear on its application. Emma fainted when the needle punctured her skin. They were able to do her blood test and chemotherapy with one puncture, and she experienced no pain when the needle was removed. Emma's newly found sense of perspective allowed her to see this as a net positive.

The endocrinologist visit was wonderful. Dr. Furlong was a genuinely nice guy, such a contrast to our last few experiences with doctors. He was able to prescribe the proper form of insulin. We had been using a different type our GP had prescribed and the new insulin came in injector pens so we didn't have to mess around with loading syringes. Emma's eyesight made it difficult for her to read the markings, she never realized she would need her glasses until she had a half full syringe in her hands. She wasn't too happy with the news she would have to take more injections daily; a dose of slow acting insulin in the morning and then fast acting insulin before each meal. The good news was she got back the freedom to eat whatever she wanted. There is no price that can be placed on freedom to eat as you wish, particularly when you love food like Emma did. She was losing about five pounds a week, and while she had never been thin, that was too much too fast.

Emma's weight quickly stabilized, and her hemoglobin, which had fallen slightly, worked its way back to normal. She hadn't lost her hair, and it was possible to believe that everything would be okay, that despite the cancer we would just walk through the rest of the treatment and live our normal lives.

✧
August 2009
✧

We entered August ending Gemzar. Emma had another CT scan to check the nodules in her lungs. There was no change, so the determination that they were not cancerous was confirmed. The positive mood generated by completing our first step was tempered by the anxiety over the next step, and this week we had two CT scans, one for the lungs and one to position the radiation tattoos. Emma had gotten herself to the point that she could drink one container of barium, and could typically get enough understanding from the technicians that they didn't hassle her much about the fact that she was supposed to drink two. It had not occurred to me that she would only drink one container **in one week.** The radiologist for her second CT was a student, and I suspect he was rethinking his career choice after Emma nearly took his head off. Talking to a woman who has been through what Emma had been through as if she were a child was a mistake he certainly never repeated. She hadn't been terribly happy about another morning at the imaging center, but she had made an attempt and nearly completed the first container of barium. Rather than accepting or understanding her situation, the young man insisted that she consume the second container. Emma was able to control herself enough that she did not throw the barium at him and simply asked for another radiologist, which was provided. She said the look on his face when his replacement showed up was worth exerting the effort of not going ballistic, and she was able to smile on the way home. It was a good thing, and we entered another vacation from treatments in a good mood.

Emma's break from hospital visits coincided with Philadelphia's first heat wave of the season, I was glad she could stay out of the heat. Even though the chemotherapy did not affect her outwardly, she was weaker, more susceptible to stress and heat. Her theories on thermodynamics and the operation of thermostats had frustrated me in the past, but I had come to the point I could accept just about anything from her, so her operation of all things to do with air conditioners and air flow in the apartment went without my interference. I wasn't able to escape the heat, my job placed me outdoors throughout the day as I traveled from one office to another. Heat is no comfort to those of us with Multiple Sclerosis, and the stress of dealing with Emma's condition and the study of the symbiotic relationships of insurance companies and hospitals was wearing on me.

We began to review the next phase, Flouricil (5fu) and radiation. For five weeks Emma would wear a pump containing a cassette of 5fu that would be infused twenty four hours a day, and she would receive radiation five days a week as well. Emma did not care for daily visits to the hospital, I did not care for the insurance company's definition of "out of pocket" expenses. If the radiation department wanted a daily copay I would need to take out a loan on my 401k. I could wait out the financial troubles, but Emma's displeasure was expressed as anger.

She was afraid. She had handled the Gemzar beautifully, but everything we could find out about 5fu suggested it was a much worse chemical. She went through all the fears about lost hair and wrinkles again, she would have to avoid sunlight, and she was already up to 8mg tablets of Dilaudid for her pain. I can never tell you enough about how strong a human being Emma was. Despite the pain, despite her fears, despite the outbursts of anger, most of the time she was a gentle, loving woman. She still expressed hope, talked about plans for the future, believed that she would survive and be healthy again.

The month ended with the beginning of 5fu. I met Janice, a nurse with the home infusion department, a year before when I had taken steroid infusions for my Multiple Sclerosis. She lived in the neighborhood and met Emma back then, so when we found that she would be Emma's home infusion nurse it was another relief. We were due for a break from the tension. The first visit went well, then we spent the week getting used to the tube running from the pump to the port. I could already see that I would be sleeping poorly for the next five weeks, I was more worried than Emma about catching the tube in my sleep or having Emma forget about the pump when she woke in the night. As it worked out Emma adapted rather quickly. By the end of the first week she was only screaming "**I CAN'T STAND THIS THING!**" once a day.

The daily radiation went better than I expected also. Of course Emma charmed the technicians, and befriended the other patients in the waiting room. Much like I feel when I visit the neurologist, Emma could see other patient's troubles as more severe than hers. She was home every morning by nine, but she was wearing thin. The chemotherapy, radiation, and Philadelphia heat were taking their toll. She still planned to walk up to Pat's Steaks on Labor Day, but she was wiped out every day after radiation, and her nausea was getting more severe. As proud of her as I was for the way she quit smoking, I had no trouble accepting that she would have to smoke marijuana to control the nausea. None of the prescribed drugs had worked, and we had gotten a wink from the oncologist who prescribed the Marinol, who said "I hear the real stuff works better".

We had one more piece of scary news. Her latest scan showed an enlarged lymph node. If it was cancer spreading during chemotherapy we were fucked. There is a finite amount of worrying that can be done.

One thing we hadn't foreseen about the pump was that when Janice came to change the needle, there would not be time to apply Lidocaine between taking out the old needle and inserting the next. Janice was very gentle, but Emma was very weak. The saving factor was that Emma was exceptionally brave.

Emma was falling into the radiation routine. She had regular friends and because she still looked and acted healthy she was an inspiration to the other patients. On Fridays she had to stop by the infusion suite for a blood test. Neither of us could figure out why they didn't just change her cassette of 5fu while she was there instead of having Janice come to our apartment, one of many departmental protocols that made no sense. The Friday before Labor Day there was no blood test scheduled, so while she was in radiation she had the technician check with the infusion department just to make sure. Twice. A few hours after she got home she received a call from the home infusion department asking why she hadn't had a blood test, and insisting she return to the hospital. Have you gotten to know Emma yet? They backed down and scheduled the blood draw for Saturday at the clinic down the street. We got up early Saturday and walked down to the clinic, where we were told there wasn't enough time to run the test and get the results to home infusion, we would have to go to the hospital. It was already miserably hot and Emma's hopes for three days without any medical attention were fluttering away. The staff at the hospital were in a hurry to get their weekend started too, so were very understanding. We were out in half an hour. By the time we got home Emma was exhausted. We laid down for a nap and missed the phone call from the infusion delivery guy, who was also in a hurry to start his holiday weekend. He left the chemotherapy and supplies on our front step. Fortunately they were neither stolen nor damaged by the heat by the time I woke up and checked the phone messages. I was about at my stress limit, so I celebrated the holiday by joining Emma in her evening smoke.

We were able to relax on Sunday, Emma was feeling well enough to go to the grocery store, one of her favorite activities. She wasn't feeling well enough to walk the extra three blocks up to Pat's Steaks, or even to eat a steak sandwich, but was hopeful enough to believe we'd go on another day. Monday I was able to see Janice when she came to change the cassette and needle. It was a nice reminder that all the hospital employees weren't robots, but the stress of the needle change without Lidocaine wiped Emma out for the day.

The heat and continued stress was affecting me, after the weekend it was almost a relief to get back to work. I didn't realize how stressed I was until I got home and found that my favorite soap opera character had been killed off. Crying for an hour was enough to convince Emma that I needed a rest, but we both knew that rest was not something either of us could offer, only comfort. She slept horribly that night, so I ended up taking the next day off and we slept together most of the day. I got to watch the soap opera, and as usual, my character had just narrowly avoided death. The week started to get a little better.

That Friday there were thunderstorms, and when Emma got to radiation she was told that they had taken a lightening strike so all radiation was canceled for the day. She went for her blood test and met with Dr. Avadhani who told Emma she was handling the 5fu well and the team remained optimistic about her progress.

About this time Patrick Swayze died of pancreatic cancer. In the same way that if you drive a red car you notice all the other red cars on the road, from the time that Emma had been diagnosed we kept hearing of other people with pancreatic cancer. Emma took the news of Swayze's death hard. He had been in the news quite a bit, and appeared to be improving when almost everyone else we had heard about had died, usually very rapidly. We knew from our own experience that each case is different, but a survival story sure would have been encouraging.

As we neared the end of the 5fu, Emma began to feel like a cancer patient. She still hadn't lost her hair or withered, and had the heat not been so intense that summer she might have made it through, but she was hitting a wall. Always tired, she was sleeping from the time she got home from radiation until I got home from work. She was too frustrated to take comfort counting down the last days of the pump, and I found myself getting used to the way the 5fu smelled. Since she spent far more time sleeping than I, I was starting to associate the scent with her, lying next to me. It was as sensual as she could be, resting, this odd coffee/ vinyl/French oak scent all over her. The love of my life was falling apart and all I could do was hold her and kiss her as she slept. I had taken to calling her "my cranky valentine", and she found a name for me, "my cheerleader from hell". It was better that she hadn't counted down the days, the 5fu and radiation was extended another few days because of the treatments she had missed when the radiation machine was down. Emma hadn't been able to take a "real" shower in over a month and just needed some creature comforts. Her extremities were starting to darken, she was dehydrated, and she had lost eight pounds over the month. Ready to quit, she needed the break to arrive.

October 2009

October began with the removal of the pump. I'm not sure what aspect Emma liked the most, but she spent almost an hour in the shower after the pump was removed. I went with her to her last few radiation treatments, but as sick as she was she put on a strong front, and some people thought that I was the patient in the couple when I accompanied her. We expected to be scheduled for surgery in about a month, so even though we knew there would be consultations and imaging, this was a break. By the end of radiation her nausea was so bad she could barely make it in for treatment, but the effects faded rapidly. She had a radiation burn on her back, but the discolored skin on her hands and feet started peeling off after a week or so. Her appetite returned, and she was able to accompany me to the grocery store by mid-month.

Now the waiting was something to trouble Emma. Where before she needed a break between appointments, now she couldn't wait for the results of the next CT scan, which would show how the treatments had affected the tumor. The day of the scan arrived. We were both so nervous that we couldn't sleep the night before. Our fried nerves received no comfort from the news that the imaging center had not received the actual prescription for the CT scan prior to our arrival. It took two hours to fax the prescription from the doctors office. My anger at the doctor faded when I found that it was due to a problem with the imaging center's fax machine. Had they just told me I could have walked over to the doctor's office and brought the prescription back.

Another week passed before we heard from Dr. Lavu with the results. We were climbing the walls. The tumor had shrunk, we would meet with Dr. Lavu the next week. It was Emma's 53rd birthday, and the other gift we received was that I managed to break my arm, putting me on disability for at least six weeks. That meant that I would be able to stay home with Emma through her surgery. It's not often you can see a broken arm as good news, but since we were also facing an impending transit strike, work would have been very difficult. Anything to reduce stress was welcome.

✧

November 2009

✧

We found ourselves adjusting to new circumstances with increasing frequency. At one point we thought Emma would be in surgery on her birthday, then mine, then Thanksgiving.

Dr. Lavu ordered additional scans with special contrasts to better illuminate blood vessels. The scans would have to be interpreted, surgery could not be scheduled until after the interpretations. Maybe days, maybe weeks. We shopped for a Thanksgiving dinner without knowing if we'd eat it, yet we were thankful. We tried not to think of things in a "This is the last time we'll . . ." way. We were hopeful, and scared. We were anxious, and afraid.

Emma continued to recover from the chemotherapy/ radiation quickly. The dark skin on her extremities had completely peeled off to healthy pink skin, the dark band in her nail bed was quickly growing out, her appetite was solid, and she gained eight pounds by mid-month. She even had a glass of wine with me on my birthday. We were enjoying our time together, the tenderness of the moments amplified by our fears. Emma still spent much of the day sleeping, and I would lie beside her, watching her face.

The special CT scan was indeed special. It was referred to in hushed tones by the technicians as "The Yeo Protocol". Emma did as she was told. The scan took two hours, during which three different contrast dyes were used simultaneously for four different scans. That Dr. Lavu would not be able to see us until December 3rd only meant that there was a lot of data to interpret. We remained thankful.

Thanksgiving was very special; we spent it alone, reflecting on the gifts of the year. We talked about all the people we had met, all the changes and challenges we had faced, the love for each other that had blossomed so beautifully. So many lives had touched ours; the chemotherapy and radiation patients whom Emma had encouraged, the technicians, nurses, and doctors who noticed and commented on her spirit. We felt proud that we had weathered this part. We knew that recovery from surgery would be a difficult time, and were thankful that my left arm had broken, that I would be able to be there with Emma and be able to take care of her. We were thankful for our friends and family, and everyone who had been there with a kind word. We were thankful for our love.

✧
December 2009
✧

We saw Dr. Lavu, he told us the surgery had been scheduled for the 11th. The tumor had shrunk, but was still around the mesenteric artery. The blood tests showed her cancer marker, CA-19-9, at a level of 25, down from 250. It was reasonable to believe that much of the remaining tumor was dead.

He went over some details about the surgery, we had read all about it and watched portions on the internet. Two surgeons would take all day to get down to the pancreas, remove the tumor, and put everything back together. Then we could expect a seven day stay in the hospital, then a month at home in bed recovering. Just about perfect timing with my time off. We were scheduled for pre-admission tests, including a PET scan (Positron Emission Tomography, straight out of Star Trek). We agreed that staying busy would be good, there was no point in idle nervousness.

The next day was cold and rainy. Joey drove us out to go shopping. Emma wanted to make gravy and freeze it so that she wouldn't have to eat my gravy. We picked up a couple of bottles of wine, one for the gravy, one for me. We found some pajamas for her to wear in the hospital, and had brunch at an IHOP where some old friends of hers worked. We mapped out the days until surgery; how we would prepare for afterward, how we would take things slow and enjoy these moments. The "last time" syndrome was unavoidable despite our certainty that Emma would survive. As we returned home the rain turned to snow, big flakes collecting on the awnings. We had planned to take a nap, but a movie I wanted to see was on. Emma actually found it interesting until the end, when it went into nonsense. Eleven years, and she never liked a movie I recommended.

The preparations were intense and precise. We were thankful we had planned ahead, tying up loose ends. Every day was filled, the day before surgery was almost ritualistic. She was on a clear liquid diet, I reserved a taxi and packed, and for some reason she decided to go online to see what the scar would look like. **Bad idea**, the site she found was of a worst case infected incision, at least we were reminded of the importance of proper wound care. In the evening I had to wash her with special cloths, a far too emotional moment for both of us, as we recognized we couldn't hold each other again until after the surgery. We hardly slept anyway, and were anxiously awaiting the taxi at 4:30 am.

The check-in went incredibly smooth. I washed her body again and helped her into her gown, took her wedding ring and necklace, kissed her, and they rolled her away by 6:30. The waiting room was comfortable, nicely designed to allow private areas; plenty of soft chairs, TVs and vending machines, electrical outlets, and internet access. I checked in with the waiting room staff, a nurse called with updates every two hours, and I spent the day updating friends by phone and internet.

Dr. Lavu came to see me at 5:00 pm, I held his hands and asked "Are these the hands that just saved my wife?". He had the expression I used to have when I faced an "impossible" task and completed it perfectly. The total time of surgery had been nine hours. Everything went well, there were no indications that the cancer had spread. They didn't expect Emma to regain consciousness that night, but I would still be able to see her in about another hour. For the second time in my life I shed tears of joy.

I was able to see Emma for about an hour that night. She was in a great deal of pain and very weak, but was still able to smile. She spoke a little, and was in good spirits, we were both so very happy that she was alive. All our unspoken fears could finally be acknowledged. She was swollen and had IVs and drains everywhere. She would be staying in intensive care for a few days.

Emma recovered quickly, but not as quickly as she would have liked. By the second day she was feeling well enough to lie to me about being cleared for fluids and even pouted when I insisted on hearing it from a nurse. Her activities started with sitting upright in a chair, and that wore her out so much she slept the next two hours. She was off oxygen and down to two IVs; with all her drains under her blanket she looked relatively healthy. In another two days she was on solid food, still in a lot of pain, but up walking and having short conversations. They put a phone in her room the fourth day, and I was able to let her talk to Autumn, our cat. Autumn had been missing her, it was good for both of them. Emma was feeling well enough to place requests with me to bring her favorite drinks to the hospital. She was still complaining of pain, but when the nurse looked into the records on Emma's pain pump, we found that she hadn't been using it as much as she could have. The machine would allow her to control her dosage of Dilaudid, but she would wait until the pain was unbearable rather than taking small doses when the pain began.

On the sixth day she had a slump. The doctors said that was normal as everything internal was starting to work again, she had just had her entire digestive tract redesigned after all. The next day she came home. She was feeling so well that by the time I got the change from the driver she was gone, leaving the taxi door standing open. She had some trouble with the stairs, it took almost half an hour for us to get to the top, but nothing was going to get between her and her own bed. She held Autumn while I went out to fill her prescriptions, when I got home they were sleeping cuddled together. Despite her tenderness we slept well that night. For the first time in a long a while we slept late.

The next day while washing her I found a bedsore. I went online and learned how to properly clean and care for that. Dr. Lavu called and said the pathology on the tumor had come back and there was no cancer present, when he heard about the bedsore he was livid. Christmas was a week away, and I already had all I could ask for.

When Christmas eventually arrived, Emma was at peace, and slept all day. I think she had set a goal of surviving until Christmas, and when she got there in one piece she was relieved. She had made preparations for a huge meal and watching a movie together, but instead she was so relaxed she collapsed. The next day it rained, and Emma was the most happy and comfortable I had seen her in as long as I could remember. She spoke to friends and family by phone, and I made the rounds to deliver Christmas presents.

My friend Sue and her sister Amy had met me for breakfast when Emma was in the hospital. Sue had given us gift certificates for Reading Terminal Market. I used them now to get supplies for New Years; cheeses and fruit and a fresh baguette. Emma had a sip of sparkling wine before we fell asleep around 9 pm. There was a sense that things would eventually return to normal. We expected it to be a long path, but we were on our way, 2010 would be the easy part.

January 2010

My wife began the year doing what she loved the most, cooking. Her energy level had bounced up and down for the last week, this morning she was feeling great. Allowing for the two hours of fireworks in the night, she had still gotten nine hours of sleep when I woke her with coffee and warm Danish pastries. She was still hungry and got up to make home fries.

Her "steri-strips", sterile cloth strips that adhere to the incision line, had all come off, and her stitches looked great. The retention sutures, sutures that held the muscles of her abdominal wall to her skin to prevent stretching the incision line, were protected outside her body with plastic tubing, and were scary looking. But her bed sore had healed completely. We spent New Years day watching marathons of Dr. Who and The Twilight Zone, exploring how intimate we could be in her condition. Cozy and warm with snow outside softening the sounds of the day, we held each other and gently made love.

Emma's recovery continued ahead of the curve, her energy increasing every day. When we saw Dr. Lavu to have the retention sutures removed, just a month after the surgery, he was amazed at how good her scar line looked. It was just a thin white line, almost invisible. Having the retention sutures removed was a huge relief for Emma. The tubes protecting the sutures were painful to roll over on during the night, and apparently they caused some tightness in her abdomen, because she felt immediate relief when they came out. She still had bad days, but when we heard an old friend of mine was having a showing of his work in a gallery in upstate New York, she was adamant about attending. The show ran through March, and she was sure she would be able to travel by then.

She wanted to get out of the house more, but with the weather her walking program was on hold. She walked up and down the stairs a couple of times a day, and wanted to go grocery shopping, but a walk to the corner store wiped her out. The exercise program Dr. Lavu had prescribed started with ten minutes of activity a day. She could see that walking to the grocery store, or even just spending an hour on her feet shopping, was beyond what was expected, but that had never stopped her before. She could rarely see her own limitations until they were reached, so I was glad to be at home to monitor her. We managed to get out before the end of the month, but only with a ride to the store and her doing nothing but shopping. She was asleep before I had everything unpacked.

As we neared the end January, and our follow up with Dr. Avadhani, Emma became nervous again. She wanted everything to be over, she'd gone through chemotherapy, radiation, and surgery. She wanted to be done. She didn't want to use her port anymore; the fact that there was a recall of the special Huber needles used to attach to the port was her sign that she should have her follow up chemotherapy through an IV in her arm. Dr. Avadhani ordered two more rounds of Gemzar, and found out that Emma had been applying the Lidocaine too late in the past, it should have been applied an hour before the puncture. That made an incredible difference and the next day when we had her port flushed she had a good visit. The port was as painless as advertised and Janice stopped by the infusion suite to visit while we were there. Emma felt great seeing her old friends, showing off her scar, and feeling important because she had a friend "in the business" to introduce to everyone. That night it snowed, and in the quiet of evening we walked down to the corner store together. She had a craving for a cherry pie, so we picked up a Tastykake cherry pie and some Ben and Jerry's "Cherry Garcia" ice cream. Dr. Lavu had told her before surgery that it would be about six weeks before she was "out and about". She found the phrase hilarious, repeating it with a Canadian accent, "Oot and aboot". In the store she looked at me, her pink wool cap tight to her head, goodies in her hands, her little triangle smile on her face, and said "Hey Blake, I'm out and about!".

That moment remains my sweetest memory of her.

I would need to get back to work soon, but those months at home with Emma were some of the most precious months of my life.

February 2010

I returned to work. I knew I needed to get back, but the time with Emma was priceless. She received the results of her latest blood work, and other than her CA-19-9 level, she was in better health than she had been last year. We had expected an increase in her CA-19-9 level; which was one reason that follow up chemotherapy was routine. We found out as everything in Emma's redesigned digestive tract moved into place it could be painful, but as long as we understood why things were the way they were, we could deal with them.

She had wanted to go out to dinner before the next round of chemotherapy. We went to Marra's again, but she lost her appetite between ordering and being served. We had everything packed and we snacked when we got back home. We were still impatient, wanting to be better than we were, pushing our limits. It was frustrating, but as soon as we took a moment to think about it, we realized that we couldn't rush this recovery.

Valentine's Day was subdued. I brought her a small box of chocolates from Godiva's. We were due to begin chemotherapy again the next day, and although we now knew that the port would be painless, there was still apprehension. Emma had waltzed through her first exposure to Gemzar, but we heard that post surgery chemotherapy could be worse due a weakened body. Emma was feeling good, but that was relative to how bad she had been. Her first dose was pushed back a week due to a snowstorm, giving us another week to worry.

This round of Gemzar did hit her harder. We took a taxi back from the infusion on Friday, and she was sick before we got home. She started to feel better late the next day, and with the steroids doing their number on her blood glucose, she was still tired on Sunday. The outside world intruded, our thermostat went out and we woke to no heat Sunday. Fortunately our landlord had spare parts, Emma slept through the repairs.

The next week we had another snowstorm, and chemotherapy was postponed again. The weather; through the heat and lightening storms that affected radiation and now the record snowfalls which were affecting chemotherapy, reminded us of our place, our tiny part in a world of over six billion people.

March 2010

Emma felt much better. With the chemotherapy working out to every other week she was recovering between doses. She dyed her hair, and we made plans to go out to breakfast on the weekend, but her reaction to the first dose wasn't a fluke, she was sick for two days again following her next treatment.

We were adjusting our expectations and schedules again. We had hoped to finish chemotherapy by our anniversary, but we were overjoyed to be having an anniversary at all. We were still figuring out what her stomach could handle, there were so many things she missed. We fully expected her to eventually have a normal diet and on her healthy days it was easy to forget that less than ninety days ago she had spent nine hours having her digestive tract redesigned.

This round of chemotherapy was bad enough for me to arrange taking off the Fridays she had treatments, in the hope that by getting her through Fridays she would be alright in time for me to go to work on the following Mondays. We adjusted the dose of slow acting insulin she took in the mornings as her blood glucose had stabilized. We tried to focus on the small victories. Then we got kicked in the teeth.

Emma's CA-19-9 level was still far too high. A normal level would have been less than 37, her latest result was 341. Dr. Avadhani scheduled a PET scan to search for any new masses. Emma was devastated. Dr.

Avadhani had prescribed Ativan as an anti nausea drug, I knew it was also used as an anti-anxiety medication. I was hoping it would help her in that way, and was considering taking it myself as we waited for the PET scan.

Spring arrived, but we didn't celebrate. While we waited for the results of the PET scan, Emma's opinion of receiving treatments returned to square one, and who could blame her? I could not bear the thought of losing her after such a brave fight, but she was resolute. No more surgeries, and since the cancer appeared to have grown through the Gemzar, chemotherapy was no longer an option. She was set on living out what remained of her life without doctors, and no amount of explaining the final stages of cancer affected her decision.

We had other issues on our minds to serve as distractions. Emma's sister in law was in the hospital with either kidney stones or cancer, and I seemed to have a hernia. Another friend had been diagnosed with colorectal cancer, and yet another was scheduled for his yearly cancer follow up, a reminder that even after surviving, you always have to keep an eye on cancer. I was scheduled for a CT scan, and Emma had her first joyful moment in a while, the thought of watching me drink the barium that she had hated so much.

We were due to see Dr. Avadhani in two weeks to discuss our options. We could figure out by the lack of rush that our situation wasn't promising. We approached our wedding anniversary knowing it would likely be our last.

April 2010

The month started with our eleventh wedding anniversary. Emma loved the commercial for Baskin Robbins ice cream cake, so I brought one home. The next day was my CT scan, and we had planned to go out for dinner, but she hadn't been sleeping all week and neither of us was up for it. We were still trying to act normal, but it was sinking in, slowly, that we weren't doing well. We were tired and scared. We needed some good news and we no longer expected it. At least her blood glucose continued to stabilize. She was down to just the one injection of slow acting insulin daily. Only rarely did she need to supplement with the fast acting insulin.

When we saw Dr. Avadhani Emma's last CA-19-9 level was 488, still moving up. The PET scan showed activity where the tumor had been, but still none in her lungs. There were clinical trails, a chemotherapy used in colorectal cancer was promising, but Emma was done. She didn't even want another blood test to see what her CA-19-9 level was that week.

We finally got out for our anniversary dinner mid-month, a nice seafood restaurant that had been in South Philly for almost a hundred years. We sat in the back, it was quiet, and our waiter was a mature gentleman who talked with Emma about their careers in the restaurant industry. Emma ate well, and was well entertained by my manipulation of crab legs. She even had a glass of wine. It was a gentle, almost normal, evening out. When we got home I held her, we hardly spoke, it was a loving and warm

45

evening. She fell asleep with her head on my chest, something she said she had never been able to do with her other husbands.

I met my old manager for lunch, he was in town for a trade show. He had just lost his father to pancreatic cancer, so we talked about the disease and the concept of hope. Glenn was a strong force in my spiritual life, whenever I lost sight of God, he could gently show me my way back. I knew that things could be much worse, I just couldn't forget how much better they had been. Glenn reminded me of the good things I still had. "Lunch" ran three hours, I put it down as educational time.

We were in no rush to see Dr. Avadhani again. We had a prescription for another PET scan, which Emma declared would be her last. She had no interest in the clinical trials, she was worn out. A year staying strong through the treatments was more than most people could pull off. She was willing to keep her appointment with the endocrinologist. Dr. Furlong was a friendly face and her diabetes was completely under control with just the one daily injection. When we saw him he told us that her A1C, a measure of average blood glucose, was perfect. She was ready to cut back on testing before every meal, there was no reason to worry about it.

May 2010

We put off getting the next PET scan. Emma's daily energy level bounced up and down, some days I'd come home and she had been out walking, some days she slept all day. She was still getting out to the computer and shopping on line. Why she felt we needed a down comforter right before summer might have triggered a discussion before, I couldn't bring myself to discuss the future anymore. We talked about the quality of our lives and reflecting on it now I realize that what we were really discussing was the quality of our love. We had not had a perfect relationship, but we had always held each other up when times were tough, and they couldn't get much tougher than they had been for the last year.

When we eventually went for the PET scan she was in a surprisingly good mood. The taxi didn't show up so we walked down to the bus stop and still got to the imaging center on time. She knew that the results of this scan would determine what was available to us, but she had already made up her mind and was just going through the motions for me. We were home by nine, and she went straight to bed. She woke up at lunch time hungry, and ate half a roast beef sandwich and some cheese fries. We watched some TV and she fell back to sleep, then woke up and ate the rest of the sandwich and some water ice. I think even if her blood glucose wasn't under control she still wouldn't have cared. She was ready to enjoy what was left of her life. She was still in a good deal of pain, and took two 8mg Dilaudid through the day, but she was still smiling, kissing me. It was some time later that I realized she wasn't just celebrating life, she was savoring it.

When we got the results of the PET scan, it showed that the cancer had spread. There was a spot in her liver now, and the spots that had been on the last scan had doubled in size. The time away from treatments had given Emma a new perspective, she was willing to go forward with the clinical trials. I was somewhat surprised, she had been against any further treatments. I thought maybe the closeness of the last few weeks had made her want to hang on. I don't think she did it just for me, not that she wasn't selfless at times. We both measured the value of treatment, the quality of any extension of her life.

We saw Dr. Avadhani a week later. It was a bad morning, noisy kids on the bus and the doctor was two hours late. Emma was ready to leave before the doctor arrived, but she stayed, probably because we both knew that if she left she would never come back. We were no longer talking about a cure, just the possibility of prolonging Emma's life expectancy from six weeks to six months. The new chemotherapy would be the colon cancer drug (Oxaliplatin) for two hours, then forty-six hours of 5fu by pump, every two weeks. The 5fu dosage would be lower than before, so it didn't seem too intrusive. We were still wary about nausea. Nothing except marijuana had any effect, and marijuana's effect was less than complete. Dr. Avadhani also gave us Oxycontin to take instead of Dilaudid at night, to help Emma sleep.

Emma seemed energized by her decision to go forward. Memorial Day weekend we went to the grocery store together so she could see her friends, unfortunately most were on vacation. We came home and had a picnic on the floor in the living room, she tried a glass of rosé but it didn't sit well on her stomach. I planned day trips between chemotherapy treatments, thinking we might get away for a weekend in Atlantic City by October. Emma was talking about next year. "Next year we'll have a real barbeque, with lobster salad and champagne". This year she made hamburgers on the stovetop; she was able to finish one before she fell asleep.

We were supposed to talk, make decisions on end of care, DNRs (Do Not Resuscitate orders), the things we hadn't discussed even before her surgery but now had to. She kept saying we'd talk about it tomorrow, and I couldn't bring myself to say to her we no longer had an endless supply of tomorrows.

June 2010

This was the most difficult month of my life, made up of several of the most difficult days of my life, and containing many of the most difficult moments in my life. We entered June believing that we could still wrestle some control, that we could pull a few more months of life out of the hat, that they would be good months. But Emma was sick. She could barely eat or drink anything without vomiting soon after. There were signs, maybe too subtle for me to notice, or maybe I just didn't want to see. She was getting to the point that I was uncomfortable leaving her at home alone. She messed up her medication one day, she could barely stay awake on a good day. The heat was so oppressive she decided to sleep on the futon in the living room, but the mattress wasn't as comfortable so she couldn't really sleep. We were both exhausted.

I took the last three days of the week off. We were supposed to go to infusion to get the chemotherapy and have the pump attached on Wednesday, then return to have it removed on Friday. Wednesday's visit was supposed to take eight hours, and as sick as she had been lately, coupled with the chemotherapy, I knew she wouldn't be alright on her own at home those days. I noticed on the bus into the infusion center that she was looking a little yellow, I don't know how long she had been this way. We typically kept the apartment dark, she had been doing all her glucose tests and her one injection each day by herself.

One year almost to the day since we were to have began chemotherapy, we were scheduled to begin this "last chance". We had an uneasy night. When we got in to the infusion center they took blood and set her up in a cubicle, then they returned with the Oxaliplatin and connected everything. They came back in five minutes to disconnect her and send us to Dr. Avadhani.

A normal bilirubin count is one. Her test the previous week had a result of four, just on the edge of being able to tolerate chemotherapy. Today it was eight. She had lost thirteen pounds in the last week, and her potassium level was extremely low. All of these symptoms could be related to a blockage in her liver, so she was scheduled for a CT scan. Hopefully an ERCP would clear the blockage that the CT scan would show. We were admitted to the hospital and she was NPO for the procedures. No beds were available in oncology, so we were set up in gastroenterology. We were hungry and in our least favorite department, the day just continued to get worse. Emma was cold and after asking for an extra blanket six times we were told that they were out. The entire fucking hospital was out of blankets? The intern who explained the procedure was less familiar with it than I was, telling us that they wouldn't need images before the ERCP. At the end of the day I left the hospital in tears, horrified that I was leaving my wife in the care of morons.

The ERCP was quick. The doctor couldn't get to the blockage. Perhaps if they had managed to perform the CT scan Dr. Avadhani had ordered they could have skipped the ERCP. Now they wanted to use CVIR (CardioVascular and Interventional Radiology, a probe forced through from outside the body). They would need an ultrasound before they could determine if CVIR would be possible. She was scheduled for the next morning, another day inpatient with no results.

The next morning as I watched the ultrasound I could swear that I saw an image of Jesus in the echoes. I'm not sure how that was supposed to be comforting, I can think of a couple of interpretations, but it did have a calming effect. We got back to the room in time to go to MRI. The cane Emma had given to me for our tenth anniversary was carbon fiber so I was allowed to keep it with me while I stayed with her, the technician had never seen a cane with no metal parts. It was 2 pm before we saw an intern who told us that the CVIR team said she wasn't a candidate and . . . "wait" . . . I interrupted here, she had been NPO since last night. "We'll talk after she can get something to eat." This is what I hated about gastroenterology, they kept forgetting that the patients were humans, with feelings and needs. They still wanted to do an ERCP, so she was **still** NPO.

They felt from what they had seen in the failed ERCP that she should have a stent placed in her duodenum because of the strictures there, thinking it would reduce her nausea. I suggested they speak to Dr. Lavu, who had created those strictures when he redesigned her digestive tract, and who we **trusted**. I emphasized the word properly, so that the intern might understand that I did not trust her. When she returned Emma had to remind her that she was in the bed, not on the floor, so she could stop looking at her shoes. We decided that this was probably the first time she had read Emma's chart and been made aware that Emma had cancer.

Later an actual doctor stopped in, when I asked him what Dr. Lavu had said about the stent he said he hadn't spoken to him, but he wanted the stent placed that afternoon. I told him that there would be no stent until I had spoken with Dr. Lavu, that Emma was no longer NPO since they would not be performing the ERCP that day, and went to the diner across the street to get her some mashed potatoes and roasted chicken. She ate lightly and fell asleep deeply.

Saturday came and the doctor who said Emma would go into immediate liver failure without CVIR now said she could wait a few days, and yet insisted he do an ERCP to place a stent in her duodenum. When I told him I hadn't heard from Dr. Lavu, he stopped bringing up the ERCP (later, when I had a chance to discuss this with Dr. Lavu, he said that he had never been contacted about an ERCP). The gastroenterology doctor then said Emma could be sent home (later, when I spoke to Dr. Avadhani, she said that her instructions had been that if an ERCP could not be done Emma was to have been released to oncology. She was in no condition to go home). **We** discovered that Emma was in no condition to go home shortly after arriving home. She was completely lost, getting out of bed and walking into walls. I was able to get her readmitted into oncology, where they took more blood samples than I had ever seen taken at one time, then took them all again from another site. She was still so out of it she didn't know she was in the hospital. I was thankful for that after her last experience.

We found that she had been released with sepsis, an infection in the blood (Dr. Klein kept calling it "blood poisoning"), so they placed her on the antibiotic Zosyn and were able to schedule a CVIR for the next morning. The results of the CVIR were immediate, she was draining a liter an hour, and even though she was taking enough Dilaudid to have the nurses double checking each time they got the order, she was clear headed again. She was tired enough to sleep through a visit from her cousin, but she asked for me to bring her robe so we could walk around the halls together. She was told she might be able to go home in a few days. Her bilirubin was at eight, it had been higher when she was admitted this time so the downward trend gave us hope that she still might be able to try the chemotherapy after she was released.

I was starting to fall into a routine and part of it was eating. With all the time I had spent in the hospital in the last week I got up to three meals a day, and while I hadn't been sleeping any better at least I was eating. There had been plenty of clues that she wouldn't, but I was still sure that Emma was going to get a little better, that she would come home, sleep in her own bed, make love, walk in the sunshine.

Emma was still having a lot of nausea, and one morning she got sick in the middle of breakfast, before I arrived. The nurse went to flush the vomit without realizing that Emma had lost her dentures, so now Emma was unable to speak. She couldn't stand being without teeth. The hospital offered to pay for a new set once she was released. She had gagged on the first casting, I had no idea how she would ever get through that process again. Fortunately it was her favorite nurse who had flushed the dentures, so she didn't stay mad. Emma always made friends with the nurses and staff, she was always bubbly and friendly, even though she was taking enough Dilaudid to knock down a horse.

Emma had been in the hospital for most of the last two weeks, and was feeling well enough to know she wanted to bathe. She was also feeling well enough to want me to give her a bath rather than the nurses. Her weight was down to 120, 60 pounds less than a year before. Her skin was dry and crackling, she was bruised at the sites where she had IVs (they ran out of veins and were using her port), she was withered from the waist up except for a swollen abdomen, and her legs were swollen. All I could see was the beautiful woman I fell in love with. We went for a walk on the floor, down to the end of the hall and back was all she could handle. The doctors thought walking would help reduce the swelling in her legs. Her blood pressure had been trending up, and I thought if we could just get home she would be able to relax.

I managed to get to the hospital early on the first day of summer. Being with Emma at the solstice for a few minutes was somehow important to me. We were still having difficulty finding something she could eat. She called me later in the day and asked that I bring watermelon, thank God for the Reading Terminal Market. She fell asleep by 6 pm and I went home early for the first time in a while. The next morning she had another CVIR. They couldn't place another drain, but flushed the ones already in place. She had called me, thirsty and scared, as I arrived at the hospital. I brought her ice chips and kissed her before she went to CVIR. We were feeling as if we were on a ride, watching without any control.

When I returned after the CVIR she was in immense pain. They were still deciding how to proceed, and since one option included anesthesia she was NPO and without pain medication, and had been all day. A new nurse came on duty and got to experience Emma at her crankiest, dinner and meds arrived shortly. They were trying a pureed diet, feeding her was too much like feeding a baby. She was becoming more and more helpless before my eyes. I told myself it was better than having her on a feeding tube. Too many of my thoughts were beginning with "It's better than . . .". There were thunderstorms that night, Emma's favorite weather, I laid alone in bed, wondering if we would ever make love again.

The next morning she looked better than I had seen her look in some time. She couldn't keep her wedding ring on anymore though. She had moved it to her thumb but as she was still wasting away, it would no longer fit there, so she gave it to me to wear. I brought her a Frosty from Wendy's on the corner. She had about two ounces and then was too full to look at dinner when it arrived an hour later. She was exhausted and fell asleep early again, while we were watching the thunderstorms through her window.

Work was slow, so I took the next day off to meet with all the doctors as they came through. She had sepsis again, this time it was fungal rather than bacterial, so they started her on a broad spectrum anti-fungal until they could identify the strain. She had blurry vision so they had an ophthalmologist stop in and check her vision. They wanted to do another CVIR, so she started the steroids in preparation for the contrast dye at noon. We were watching thunderstorms through her window, the wind-swept rain across the rooftops around us was beautiful, when Dr. Avadhani stopped by.

It was clear where the conversation was going. Even in the depths of denial the truth continues to exist. Emma needed to be helped into the bathroom, so Dr. Avadhani and I spoke together in the hallway. Emma's bilirubin was back in the high eights, maybe the CVIR would help, maybe it was the sepsis. Her CA-19-9 level was in the thousands. I could see pain in Dr. Avadhani's eyes, she could see tears in mine. We had been talking about her pregnancy, the life she was bringing into the world, and now she has told me my wife is dying and there's nothing we can do

except make her comfortable. When Emma went home she would be in
the care of Hospice. We've handled all this better than other patients. We
pursued an aggressive course of treatments, we had encouraging results,
we did our best. I felt worse for Dr. Avadhani than I did for us. She said
goodbye to Emma, and as the storm cleared, we tried to process the
information.

I stopped by in the morning, and escorted Emma to radiology for her
CVIR. The technician asked if I was her son, people used to think we
were siblings. The CVIR was very productive. Emma was being returned
to her room when I arrived that afternoon. While they were settling
her in they emptied a liter and a half from the drains. An hour later they
took another liter. Her abdomen looked like a fallen soufflé. She was still
groggy but hungry, she ate about four ounces of pureed meatloaf and fell
asleep.

The next day she was sitting up in a chair and very alert when I arrived.
She was in good spirits, but still couldn't keep anything in her stomach,
not even water. Her potassium level was now too high. She said the
medication tasted like pineapple, I thought it was more like nail polish
remover. She couldn't keep it down either, so they had to give her the
medication rectally. Maybe it was some near death euphoria, but she
remained cheerful, making jokes about our sex life when they had to
give her the medicine. We talked more than we had in weeks. I had to
explain to the nurse that even though the swelling in her legs had gone
down, they were still twice the diameter they had been when we entered
the hospital. Where her abdomen had been swollen it was now bruised.
The drain was slowing down, she was scheduled for another CVIR

on Monday, so she would be in the hospital until the Fourth of July weekend.

As much as I wanted her to come home, as much as **she** wanted to come home, I was worried about her coming home on a holiday weekend. I was worried that she might not be ready, and would have to be rushed back to the hospital with short staff and the traffic that comes with Independence Day in Philadelphia. I spoke to my mother about it on the phone, and she said "What would you come back to the hospital for?" I had allowed myself not to think about what Hospice and Palliative care were. I forgot what I had told myself and everyone else, that she just wanted to spend **one more night** in her own bed, with Autumn by her side. The fight was over, yet I wasn't letting go. How could I when she was alive, laughing, kissing me each day?

At the end of the hallway was a waiting room, a bridge connected this floor to maternity in the building next door. I used the bridge as a place to make phone calls. As I returned to Emma's room I stopped and was talking to the father of one of the delivering mothers. He was a little younger than I, his second grandchild arriving on his first grandchild's third birthday, so the family was divided between celebrations. Somehow the contrasts were comforting, life goes on.

The weekend had the added stress of Emma's unbalanced brother having one of his "episodes". Every night when I returned home there would be several phone messages from him or one of his immediate family, filth from sick minds. They were threatening to come to the hospital; unlikely since they never crossed the river, but to be avoided at all costs. I had to change the home phone number and have Emma moved to a room under a "no information" order. No one could even find out if she was a patient at the hospital. With no visitors and no phone calls, Emma's blood pressure dropped to normal in two days. Maybe he did us a favor.

No one had ordered steroids for Emma's CVIR, so it was postponed until Tuesday, then postponed again because her platelets were low. All the things we've learned in the hospital! There's something called FFP, Freshly Frozen Plasma, that she received to bring up her platelet count. The FFP was more closely controlled and monitored than the opiates. A team of two technicians administered it with the precision of a moon launch.

I ran home during the CVIR to get a new belt for the vacuum, I was busy preparing the house for Emma's return. She was totally zonked when I got back. I stayed until I knew she was asleep for the night. The next morning she appeared much better, the new drain was productive and they started her on Lasix to reduce the swelling in her legs. She still couldn't keep anything down, but her eyes still sparkled. The woman I loved was still there, and we believed that she could make it home. Our expectations had been pared. We had entered the hospital thinking we could get another six to eight months. Then we hoped for just a few months. At this point we still thought we had weeks.

July 2010

Emma called early. I was still getting ready for work. The team of doctors on her case was to meet with us today, to discuss palliative care. Emma didn't know what they meant. She had thought they said "elective care". I knew this was coming, I had quickly put it to the back of my mind when I spoke with Dr. Avadhani the week before. Emma was still channeling Rocky Balboa, talking about how she was going to beat cancer. She defined survival as completely defeating the disease, I defined survival as weathering the storm with grace. She was so strong, surviving on the force of her will, but her body wasn't cooperating, no matter how hard her spirit fought. I wanted to hold her and make love, and I was afraid of hurting her fragile body. I spent some time alone crying for what I had lost, and what I was losing.

The team gathered in her room. A new doctor was taking over for Dr. Klein on the oncology floor. We discussed what palliative care meant. Even when you've heard something several times, had it thrust in your face, and think you've understood and processed it, it can still be news. Dr. Klein made references to the Alamo, I must have worn my "Don't Mess with Texas" shirt on the weekends.

The primary life-threatening issue was the blood infection. The infection could be held at bay with the antibiotics and antifungals, but the source of the infection was the blockage in her liver. As long as the bile could not drain properly, the infection(s) would continue to thrive. The biliary tree, the branches through which the bile flows, had multiple obstructions. We could go through several CVIR procedures, but what was causing the obstructions was the cancer, which continued to flourish. There was no way to slow down the cancer, any treatments would require her liver to be functioning properly. That left us taking antibiotics and antifungals until the cancer shut down her liver. We could do that at home. I could stop worrying about her getting any worse, she was.

There was no way to say if she had days or weeks, but months was out of the question. I kept thinking of Dr. Martin Luther King Jr.'s last speech, "Well, I don't know what will happen now; we've got some difficult days ahead. But it really doesn't matter with me now, because I've been to the mountaintop. And I don't mind. Like anybody, I would like to live a long life—longevity has its place. But I'm not concerned about that now. I just want to do God's will." Emma had been my mountaintop, she had shown me elements of life that were hidden before. I would indeed like to live a long life, but without Emma, that really didn't matter to me now. I just wanted her to be happy and comfortable. After that didn't concern me. How could I make plans that depended on her death? I made plans; to do things with Emma. We even thought we would be allowed time enough to squeeze some of those things in that summer, but those plans were dust. That was God's will.

We aimed for Emma to return home on Tuesday, July 6th.

Friday Dr. Kelly, Dr. Klein's replacement, was pushing for Emma to go home ASAP. I'd heard this song before in gastroenterology. I wasn't sure if he was trying to empty a bed, or if he was trying to help, wanting to fulfill her wish to die at home. I felt paralyzed. We had come to an agreement at the meeting that she would go home on Tuesday, did he no longer think she would live that long?

Emma spent the day calling friends and saying goodbye. She didn't want visitors at home. There were a few people she wanted to see before she left the hospital and then she wanted to be left alone.

Dr. Lavu stopped in. We all held hands. He had tears in his eyes. Emma's Aunt Anna and Cousin Lorraine stayed a few hours. She called her friend Catherine, but as usual Catherine couldn't shut up long enough to listen to what Emma was trying to tell her. Emma just shook her head as she hung up the phone, Catherine would never change, and on some level that brought Emma comfort as well.

I woke early Saturday morning. More accurately, I didn't sleep, and got tired of screaming into the pillow. It was happening today, she was coming home, and it didn't matter that it was the holiday. She would sleep in her home, with her cat and her husband by her side, and she would die. There was no going back to the hospital, the crises could not be avoided. We were no longer talking about **when**, we were talking about **where**.

Our landlords visited at the hospital, David and Jackie were more like family. They sent money for groceries when she was first sick and paid for us to go out for dinner on our anniversary. This day they brought a plant, a "Crown of Thorns". Emma and I had a variant of the species that she kept going our entire marriage, even sharing with friends cuttings

that had grown to be bushes. She loved the flowers that she could
magically coax our plant to produce year round.

Emma decided she needed to follow Dr. Kelly's plan, so we were aiming
to go home Sunday, July 4th. There was a lot to coordinate, and being
the Saturday of a holiday weekend, it was a little frustrating dealing with
the various departments that would be handling her care. Bouncing
between them, I was starting to feel like I was on a roller coaster. She was
declining rapidly. At one point the nurse thought she had wet the bed,
but it was the fluid from her legs leaking through her skin. She vomited
green beans, which she had consumed four days before. Her digestive
system had shut down.

Sunday I spoke with the hospice nurse and received Emma's durable
equipment before I went to the hospital. There were several questions
about care, and she said she'd get back to me. The doctors were planning
a 1 pm release. When I hadn't heard back from hospice by 1130 am,
I brought the doctors up to speed on the various preparations or lack
thereof. The issue at hand was the balancing of the various hospice
and home care agencies. Emma couldn't take anything orally, so her
antibiotics and pain medication would have to be administered IV (I
was trying not to think about nutrients, or the fact that no one else
was thinking about them either). Home care doesn't run IVs, so they
had handed her case over to home infusion. Home infusion **only** runs
IVs, and Emma needed more than just an IV. I still thought she would
live long enough to need more. The doctors decided the coordination
of services would take a few more days. She couldn't be released yet.
I wanted to have a pharmacy right down the hall while they were

coordinating the services, Emma just wanted to go home. Neither of us were certain that she would make it home at all.

That morning, when we still thought we were going home that day, Emma turned down her sponge bath. She wanted me to bathe her after we got home. She told the nurse she missed my touch. She just wanted a few simple things, her bed, her cat, her husband. Her husband just wanted to have one morning waking by her side. Through all of this Emma remained alert, at least when she was conscious. She kept her sense of humor, the nurses were amazed by her. When they needed to increase her medication to keep up with the pain, I was afraid we were going to lose that alertness. I didn't know if she would know that she was home if she got there. I had to get her home for her, and I needed her home myself, even if it was just for one more night.

For the first time I spent the night at the hospital. Our nurse, Suzanne, helped with the arrangements. Emma had charmed Suzanne, as she had always charmed people. Suzanne asked about attending Emma's memorial services, and the immediacy of the request didn't strike me. Everyone had wanted to memorialize Emma. Later I realized that Suzanne had suspected she wouldn't see Emma again. I **still** did not accept how little time was left. I told Suzanne about Emma's wishes; that there be no services, that she be cremated, she didn't even want an urn. She just wanted me to keep her ashes in a cardboard box. Suzanne smiled, yes, that would be what Emma would want. I was able to talk Emma into allowing me to put her ashes in an urn, and her cousin Lorraine had gotten Emma's permission to dedicate a mass to her no sooner than six months after her death. All Emma desired was that people remember her, that they raise a glass in her memory. No one who ever met Emma could ever forget her.

We were quiet most of the day, she didn't want the TV on. She mostly slept, I sat at her side, holding her hand, studying her face. Her level of pain was increasing hourly. I was thankful for the pharmacy down the hall. Around 9 pm she woke up and wanted the TV on. We watched the fireworks and a concert on the Parkway, some hip hop band with a guy playing the sousaphone jumping all over the stage. As surreal as that image seemed to my sober mind, I wondered what went through Emma's mind. They were alternating Dilaudid and morphine in her IV in addition to giving her morphine lollipops. Each hour required new approvals for the incredible doses she was receiving. Her kidneys failed. She felt the need to urinate due to the swelling in her abdomen, but the little hand-held ultrasound device showed her bladder was empty. She wanted to get up and sit on the toilet, but her legs were so swollen that we could barely move her. Her blood pressure was dropping. I asked if there was something that should be done about it. The nurse looked at me with the softest expression and said "It's part of the process". Emma was still making jokes with the nurses, I could see that they were amazed that she was laughing, not from the drugs, but from her joy of life.

About 5 am she looked at me and I could feel her hand tighten in mine, she didn't have the strength to squeeze me. She said "I can't fight anymore". I watched her eyes close. I stayed bent over her, my face close to hers, feeling her weak breath on my face. I told her that our time apart would seem like an instant from the perspective of eternity, reminded her of God's promise of eternal life, and quoted bible verses. I kissed her neck, her breasts, her hands, her face. At about 6 am she stopped breathing. I might have screamed. The nurses came in, I looked up at them and quietly said "I think she's gone". There was no rush. One nurse checked for a pulse. I told them we never filled out a DNR. They didn't seem to care, so either they were more up to speed on their hospice role than I was, or Emma had filled out the form without telling me.

The nurses were very kind. I stayed with Emma, holding her hand, while I called friends and family. Due to the hour and the holiday I spoke mostly to answering machines. The priest on duty stuck with the Catholic practice of ignoring the dead, but sent an Episcopalian seminary student to speak with me. We joked about Catholics. Emma's Aunt Anna came in and I gave her the necklace Emma always wore. It had been a gift from Emma's mother, Anna's sister.

When the time came to wash Emma's body rigor mortis had set in, her hand was stiff and still curled around mine. I washed her, gently caressing the body that had once been so full of life, now just an empty container. I stroked her hair and kissed her face and neck, I made earplugs for her from a tissue that I had used for my tears, Emma had always slept with paper earplugs. As I put them in her ears I whispered to her "This is the last time we'll share bodily fluids". She would have found that statement hilarious. Then I helped place her body into the bag and onto the gurney.

They go to great lengths to hide death in the hospital, there was a special gurney that had a table top over her body that they draped a sheet over, it looked like a catering table as they rolled her away, so ironically fitting for her.

I packed her things, including the plant she had received just two days earlier.

Anna waited down the hall while Emma was washed and removed. Anna's son Brian picked us up and drove us home. I felt like the character Mathilda from the movie "Leon" as I walked out of the hospital, a bag of Emma's belongings on my shoulder, my cane in one hand, the plant in the other. When I came home I found the house arranged for Emma's return; the futon made out and covered with Chux.

I began the arrangements for her cremation, Nunzio Carto had handled all her family's funerals. He and Emma had a romantic episode long ago and she had been adamant that he not be alone with her corpse. I figured she was safe for the ride to the crematory. Lorraine helped me choose the urn, pink with a dark rose, everyone agreed that Emma would have loved it. I realized I hadn't eaten in a while, so I grabbed a sandwich, then I realized I hadn't slept in a while and collapsed on the futon. The Chux seemed to weigh too much to move them. I couldn't enter the bedroom.

The next days were spent keeping occupied with details. I arranged to see a grief counselor, choosing a woman who had an office near the Curtis building so that I could visit the mural "Dream Garden". This glass mosaic by Louis Comfort Tiffany was designed by Maxfield Parrish, two of our favorite artists. I split up the fruit basket from the office with my downstairs neighbor Abby. I made some trips around the neighborhood to share the news. We had breathed this neighborhood together for the last seven years. Every bump in the sidewalk had some memory of Emma connected to it. Most people were shocked. She had never appeared to be sick, and their grief reminded me of how she touched people so deeply. A few were rude, reminding me of how Emma could get along with all sorts.

It's hard to say what normal behavior is, I built a shrine for Emma in the living room, a tall glass display case with her urn and some special items, memorabilia from her life and careers. I included the box of photos of her first husband and a stuffed toy she used to chase Autumn with. When I received her ashes I had to touch them and taste them, we had an incredibly sensual relationship. Then I placed her loose gemstones with her ashes, or "cremains" as they're properly called. I placed her urn in the shrine. I still talk to her.

It took a few days to enter the bedroom, and weeks before I slept there. Autumn stayed by my side. We took her in as a feral kitten and she identified with Emma as her mother. She used to suckle on Emma's clothing, never mine. One night she started suckling on my shirt. It gave me another reason to cry. Every time I was on the phone Autumn would climb all over me, thinking Emma was on the other end. We had always put Autumn on the phone when one of us called.

Over the next weeks I cleaned the apartment. I had stocked up on things she could eat, then the next things she could eat, then at the end things for when she came home, so the pantry was packed. I found out the first time I cooked that Emma had been placing the pans in the oven instead of washing them the week before she went into the hospital. There was a mountain of paper earplugs on her side of the bed. I took most of her clothes to the Salvation Army and kept a few intimate things, planning to make a pillow out of them.

My eldest daughter stopped by one weekend. I hadn't seen her in years. My father made his yearly visit a week or two later. We went for dinner to a restaurant Emma had always wanted to visit, I had a glass of her favorite wine. My youngest son stopped on his way through town, a gentle giant of a man. It was wonderful to see him. Emma's family had never been close, but I stayed in touch with them, and all the distant relatives who I had come into contact with around Emma's death, for a few months.

My grief counselor said Emma and I had mourned for the year she was sick, and that was why I handled her death so well. I'd sure hate to see someone who wasn't handling it well. I think I just put up a good front. While she was in the hospital several people told me how strong I was. Definitely a good front.

I received cards and emails of condolence and support from friends and family around the world. One internet friend, a man I never met in person, sent C.S Lewis' book "A Grief Observed", possibly the most helpful thing I read during this period. A number of people asked if there was anything I needed. I avoided the obvious answer. I would say "I don't know what I need". I knew then and I know now. I needed Emma. There was no one who could give her back to me.

I made attempts to socialize, went to one friend's fiftieth birthday with a crowd of old friends I hadn't seen in years. No one noticed that I had only sent my body. I made plans for a trip to Massachusetts, to a B&B that Emma would have loved. I visited a friend from high school and her sister, who convinced me that based on her own experiences, life doesn't end when your spouse dies.

Among the condolence cards was the occasional get well card for Emma. There is no way to measure which was more likely to snap my heart. I was asked immediately if I planned to remarry. The question was a total shock. I couldn't imagine putting another woman in the position of "replacing" Emma. Still laughing at my insistence that I could make plans, God sent the most incredible woman to me just a few weeks later. I was remarried before the end of the year.

Life does go on. It hasn't been a year since Emma died. I'm remarried, relocated, starting a new career and I'm still mourning. I don't know how long it will last. Most days are filled with light, and the memories that come from everywhere make me smile. Some days I miss her so much I can't stand it and can't stand that I've tried to live without her. She is in the fabric of my soul. She is part of who I am, but I am also more. As I went through some belongings I was reminded that I had an entire life before I met Emma. I am allowed to have one after her.

21 June 2011, Princeton, NJ

About the Author

K. Blake Cash witnessed the daily effects of pancreatic cancer and cancer treatments during his wife's fourteen month battle with the disease. "Surviving" is the story of their journey, from diagnosis through the loss of his wife. He used the website he created to record her struggle and eventually memorialize her in the creation of this book. Mr. Cash continues to redefine surviving today as a writer, living in Princeton NJ with three cats, two step teenagers, and his very supportive new wife.

A portion of the proceeds from the sale of this book will go towards funding Emma's website (http://blakeandemma.mysite.com) and contributions to the Pancreatic Cancer Action Network.

CPSIA information can be obtained at www.ICGtesting.com
Printed in the USA
270265BV00005B/41/P